first book about animals

of the polar regions

For a free color catalog describing Gareth Stevens'
list of high-quality books and multimedia programs,
call 1-800-542-2595 (USA) or 1-800-461-9120 (Canada).
Gareth Stevens Publishing's Fax: (414) 225-0377.

Library of Congress Cataloging-in-Publication Data available upon
request from publisher. Fax: (414) 225-0377 for the attention of
the Publishing Records Department.

ISBN 0-8368-2652-3

This North American edition first published in 2000 by
Gareth Stevens Publishing
1555 North RiverCenter Drive, Suite 201
Milwaukee, WI 53212 USA

© QA International, 1999
Additional end matter © 2000 by Gareth Stevens, Inc.

Created and produced as *visit the animals
in the polar regions* by QA International,
329 rue de la Commune Ouest, 3e étage,
Montréal, Québec, Canada H2Y 2E1.
Tel.: (514) 499-3000 Fax: (514) 499-3010
www.qa-international.com

Printed in the United States of America

1 2 3 4 5 6 7 8 9 04 03 02 01 00

Gareth Stevens Publishing
MILWAUKEE

The penguin is not afraid...

2

of the cold.

The beluga whales...

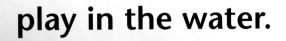

play in the water.

The polar bear is walking...

6

on the ice floe.

The prehistoric mammoth shows...

its two, long tusks.

The snow leopard is watching...

the snowflakes fall.

The musk ox is wearing...

its warm fur coat.

The arctic fox...

loves the winter.

Glossary

afraid — scared; full of fear.

arctic — of the region around the North Pole.

beluga — a white whale.

floe — a large, flat mass of floating ice.

mammoth — a large type of elephant with long, curved tusks and thick body hair that lived a long time ago. Mammoths no longer exist.

prehistoric — from a time long ago, before people began to keep written records.

tusks — long, pointed teeth that are used for digging or as a weapon.

Index